Original title:
Beneath the Roof of Time

Copyright © 2025 Creative Arts Management OÜ
All rights reserved.

Author: Julian Montgomery
ISBN HARDBACK: 978-1-80587-099-9
ISBN PAPERBACK: 978-1-80587-569-7

Tidal Waves of History

In the tide of days gone by,
Fish take naps, dreams float high.
Rabbits wearing old top hats,
Chuckle 'neath the oncoming chats.

Calendars dance with silly feet,
Telling tales of backseat heat.
Tick-tock clocks join the parade,
Waving hands in rhyming cascade.

Mice in suits on tiny bikes,
Zooming past with all their likes.
History's a wobbly game,
Playing charades without the fame.

So let's toast with mugs of stew,
Laughter echoes, history's brew.
In every giggle, every jest,
Time reveals its zanni best.

Conversations with a Pendulum

Tick-tock, what a bore,
Swinging back and forth once more.
"What's your secret?" I did ask,
"Just hang around, it's quite my task!"

With every tick, it seemed to grin,
"I watch the folks, that's where I win!"
A wise old weight, stuck in a clock,
"I'm just here for the classic mock!"

Portraits of Fleeting Tomorrows

Snapshots of the future's fun,
Where laughter rises like the sun.
Each second giggles, spinning dreams,
And life's not quite what it seems.

Painted smiles on frames so wide,
Time's a jester, full of pride.
With every brush, we twist and bend,
In these moments, never end.

Windows to Another Era

Peering through those glassy panes,
The past chuckles, drops its chains.
What's that smell? Oh, popcorn's popping!
Is it history? Oh, that's hopping!

With each glance, a bright surprise,
A dance of socks and silly ties.
Funny hats and strange old shoes,
Through those frames, I binge my views!

The Gentle Weight of Wednesday

Wednesday wears a cozy hat,
Calls out to me, "Hey, how about that?"
A midweek laugh, a tickle here,
Says, "Two more days 'til weekend cheer!"

She struts along with all her flair,
Winks at Thursday, says, "I dare!"
A gentle tug, a playful tease,
In her lightness, life's a breeze!

The Gentle Passing of Hours

Tick tock, the clock dances by,
Like a cat chasing butterflies.
Minutes flip like pancake dreams,
Waffle hours, or so it seems.

Time spills tea, then makes a snack,
Juggling where the moments lack.
A nap in a hammock, oh so nice,
While seconds sprinkle in a slice.

Unraveling Threads of Time

A sweater knit from days of yore,
Pulled by toddlers, it's quite a chore.
Button memories fall and roll,
Knitting past, it has control.

Yarn in tangles, laughter waits,
Spaghetti days and twisting fates.
We stitch our tales with playful glee,
Dancing in time's great tapestry.

Rooms that Remember

In corners where the dust bunnies play,
Old socks plot schemes to run away.
The fridge hums tunes of past delights,
Whispering secrets, well into nights.

Chairs creak with gossip from the past,
Sharing jokes that never last.
Walls giggle, covered in strange art,
As echoes of laughter fill every part.

Flickers of Long-Ago Laughter

Ghosts of chuckles in candlelight,
Ballet dancing on a starry night.
Echoes of pranks that never die,
Flickering joy that makes us sigh.

Flashback chuckles, a comic spree,
Joking with shadows, wild and free.
Time-traveling jokes, how they soar,
A punchline wrapped in forevermore.

Relics of the Past

Old socks on the line, waving good day,
Dancing with ghosts, in a silly ballet.
The toaster's a time machine, it's so quite rare,
With burnt toast reminders of breakfast despair.

Grandma's vase winks, it's been through a lot,
With stories of blunders, it recalls each plot.
We laugh at the tales held in porcelain glare,
As time gives a chuckle, it just doesn't care.

Flickering Flames of Memory

Remember that prank with the flickering flame?
A candle that danced when it heard its own name.
It melted away all our fears of the night,
Yet left us with wax toys that gave quite a fright.

Those moments we laughed, oh, how time flew by,
With shadows that winked in the candlelight sky.
We swore we'd remember each giggle and glee,
But now we just chuckle—what was that memory?

The Weight of Hours

The clock on the wall weighs more than a ton,
It ticks like a drum, like an oversized gun.
Each hour a step, we're marching in place,
In this silly parade, we're losing the race.

Time wears a costume, all frilly and bright,
With pockets of laughter, it shrinks into night.
We run after moments, oh what a pursuit,
With seconds like sprinters in fanciful boots.

A Lantern for Lost Things

With a lantern that shines for things lost and missed,
We hunt for that sock in a whimsical tryst.
It flickers and giggles, it teases the dark,
A scavenger's dream with a comical spark.

Old toys lay slumbering, waiting to play,
While memories frolic, they laugh and they sway.
A sock finds a partner, their dance starts anew,
As we chuckle along with the things we outgrew.

The Library of Unseen Moments

In dusty shelves, a sock resides,
Forgotten tales and silly slides.
A feathered hat from days of yore,
Winks at us from its hidden store.

A cat that reads while sipping tea,
Dances with a ghost, oh what glee!
The clock just chuckles, can't be late,
Time's just a joke, it's all first-rate!

Timeless Murmurs in the Attic

Old photos giggle, they know the score,
Pants from the '80s, who wears those anymore?
Marbles roll like whispers on the wood,
Laughing secrets where no one stood.

A moth in glasses, reading a book,
Winks knowingly with every look.
Dust bunnies host their own little show,
While cobwebs weave tales of long ago.

Whispers of Hours

Time plays tricks, just like my shoelace,
Trips me up when I'm in a race.
Tick-tock clocks can't stop their play,
Each second giggles, come what may.

In the corner, a chair starts to sing,
Of lost hobbies and a missing ring.
Remote controls that vanish with fright,
While socks escape into the night.

Shadows in the Attic

Skeletons laugh in the cupboard's gloom,
Worn-out shoes who've danced with doom.
A rollicking laugh echoes with pride,
As the old broom takes its joyride.

The past prances in mismatched shoes,
Spilling secrets like delightful news.
While whispers flutter like worn-out maps,
Guiding mischief in tricky traps.

Whispers of Ages Past

In shadows of the yesteryears,
Echoes of laughter dance with cheers.
A relic talks of socks once lost,
From battles fought, and what they cost.

A hat that spins a tale or two,
Of windy days and skies so blue.
It chuckles softly, 'Where's my friend?'
As socks and shoes begin to blend.

Echoes in the Attic

Up in the attic, dust bunnies play,
They throw crazy parties every day.
Forgotten toys join in with glee,
While old books sigh, 'Oh, let us be!'

The clock strikes twelve, and off they go,
Chasing each other, to and fro.
An old coat jokes 'I'm still in style,'
While cobwebs laugh, their crafty wile.

Shadows on the Ceiling

In the room, shadows wiggle and dance,
Each one sporting its own little prance.
The cat looks up, confused and astute,
Wondering if they'll make a cute pet.

A shadow of socks strikes a pose,
While forgotten dreams take off their clothes.
The light dims low, it's time for a break,
As the shadows begin to giggle and shake.

The Threads that Bind Us

Threads from the past weave stories anew,
Of stitches and snags that never quite grew.
A button pops, and what a surprise,
As laughter erupts and echoes in skies.

Old photographs wink with a smile,
As fading memories dance in style.
'Remember that time?' they collectively say,
While scarves ensnare hats that roll away.

Glimmers of Lost Futures

In a jar, I trapped a dream,
But it rolled out, like a cream.
Time's a joker, with a grin,
Spilling laughs where woes have been.

Clock hands dance like silly fools,
Tick-tocking over broken rules.
Yesterday's fashion, quite absurd,
I wore it proud, as I interred.

Futures glimmer in a jar,
What they'll become? O, who knows far?
But each giggle is a sign,
That silly paths are truly fine.

Time's a laughter, come and see,
Waltzing through absurdity.
Shadows cast, with a wink so sly,
Holding secrets that fly high.

A Soliloquy of Timelines

I once dated a calendar date,
But it ghosted me – how rude, that fate!
Plans mislaid like missing socks,
Time just plays games with paradox.

Memories knock on my brain's door,
Asking for snacks and wanting more.
Strange timelines blend in this charade,
Two timelines, one ice cream parade!

Chronicles bent, like a silly straw,
Laughter echoes in each faux pas.
Past and future share a seat,
With each tale, life takes a beat.

I tripped on hours, slick as oil,
In the garden of time's great toil.
With all my flops, I take a bow,
A comedian's grace is all I vow.

The Archive of Echoing Steps

I walked on clouds made of pancake fluff,
Collecting echoes, that's enough!
Steps were slappy, in a merry beat,
Squirrels joined in, what a feat!

Rolled up memories, like old receipts,
Dance in the room with silly feats.
Each step a giggle, a tale exchanged,
In the archives, all rearranged.

Retrospective, what a view,
Time's a prankster, it's true!
Collecting giggles like jars of jam,
Slippery stories of who I am.

Echoes laugh, bounce off the walls,
Footsteps tangle and weave in stalls.
In the hallway of laughter divine,
Every misstep is a punchline.

The Lost Art of Remembering

Remember when I forgot my name?
Grabbed a noodle and played a game.
My brain was a sieve, it made me sigh,
But laughter helps my thoughts to fly.

Papers pile, oh what's this mess?
Where's that recipe for happiness?
Forgot my keys, left out the pie,
Yet in my heart, the joys comply.

I tried to remember my uncle's cat,
Instead, I recalled a funny hat.
Memories play hide-and-seek,
In silly corners, where they peek.

Art of recalling is quirky fun,
Time pulls tricks, we're never done!
With every giggle, a tale unfolds,
In the gallery of laughter, life molds.

Memories in the Dust

In the attic, old shoes lie,
Next to hats that wave goodbye.
Dust bunnies hold a grand parade,
While grandma's slippers start to fade.

Oh, the things we used to wear,
Mismatched socks - a fashion dare!
Couches that squeak when we sit,
Whispers of laughter that won't quit.

Old toys with tales they spin,
Squeaky voices hiding within.
An ancient clock begins to chime,
Tick-tocking all our silly time.

Memories layer thick like fluff,
In cozy corners, just enough!
We stumble upon joy misplaced,
In dusty treasures, time embraced.

Time's Silent Watcher

A clock with hands that dance so slow,
Watches us put on a show.
It chuckles as we race and run,
While seconds giggle in the sun.

Cups of tea spill tales untold,
Of silly antics, brave and bold.
Time winks as we fumble around,
In life's circus, we're all clowns.

Old chairs creak with every joke,
While the cat just yawns and spoke.
It knows the punchlines, oh so well,
In this bizarre, little carousel.

Hours stretch like lazy cats,
While we chase after silly spats.
Yet every tick, a wink we find,
In the chaos, we're unconfined!

Chronicles of the Hearth

The fireplace crackles with delight,
As marshmallows take a lofty flight.
Ghosts of pizzas long devoured,
Dance with crumbs, they feel empowered.

The kettle whistles, loud and clear,
Teasing us with steaming cheer.
Grandpa claims it's magic brew,
That turns time silly, just like glue!

We gather 'round, our stories flair,
Each one ending with a stare.
Laughter bounces off the walls,
Time's playful echo never stalls.

In this cozy, playful space,
Time's quirks we always embrace.
With every joke and every rhyme,
We dance together, defying time.

Fleeting Moments in a Jar

Captured giggles gather dust,
In jars where memories adjust.
Each whiff of laughter, a sweet breeze,
Poking fun at life's unease.

Strawberries floating in a dream,
Dance in syrup, a playful theme.
Sunshine smiles, all bottled tight,
Ready to pop out, just for a bite.

In the pantry, silliness brews,
While we cherish the wacky hues.
A sprinkle of chaos, a dash of fun,
Moments in jars, forever spun.

Grandma's cookies, a time machine,
Taste of laughter, a sweet routine.
As we munch on carefree delights,
Time's fleeting winks become our flights.

Faded Colors of Dusk

The sun dips low, it yawns and sighs,
A canvas splashed with sleepy skies.
Cats parade in twilight's glow,
While squirrels plot a comical show.

The breeze a chuckle, soft and sly,
Tugging hats that float on high.
Laughter lingers in the air,
As shadows play without a care.

Old folks nod off, heads in a spin,
Dreams of dancing, they begin.
Stars peek out, their smirk is wide,
In the fading light, we all abide.

As dusk descends, a wink is made,
Colors blush, but none betrayed.
The day wraps warmth in humorous glee,
In the palette of night, we find esprit.

The Creak of History

A floorboard squeaks, a ghost alludes,
Echoes laugh in old attitudes.
Dusty tales in corners hide,
Where socks and secrets coincide.

Grandpa's chair gives a snarky creak,
It knows the jokes we dare not speak.
Portraits wink with stories bold,
While tales of mishaps are retold.

Time's a jester in the hall,
With every tick, it has a ball.
Silly whispers paint the day,
As history dances in disarray.

The clock strikes funny, round and round,
A giggle echoes as we're bound.
In creaks and chuckles, joy we find,
With mischief lurking left behind.

Moments Caught in Woodgrain

In every knot, a tale resides,
Of silly falls and joy that glides.
Grains like laughter, twist and twine,
Whisper secrets, oh how they shine!

The table holds our wobbly feast,
Where every laugh brings out the least.
Spills and thrills escape the cup,
As memories swirl, we lift them up.

Chairs wobble, greet our playful sway,
Caught in moments, they dance and play.
Woodgrain sings with every crack,
As we share stories, never lack.

Time paints smiles in every line,
Laughs like echo, sweet as wine.
In every scratch, in every stain,
Happiness blooms, again and again.

Dance of the Dust Motes

In sunlit beams, they twirl in flight,
  Tiny dancers in delight.
Spinning round on air so sweet,
  Party time for the small elite.

With giggles soft, they mock our toil,
  They seem to flourish in old soil.
Amidst the clutter, they play a game,
  While we are busy, all the same.

Dust bunnies chuckle, the cobwebs glide,
  The world's a stage, they take in stride.
A whimsical waltz, sets hearts aglow,
  As time winks at this joyful show.

In lazy afternoons, they bind us tight,
  With laughter caught in golden light.
So let them dance, let them elate,
  For in their joy, we all await.

The Soundtrack of Shadows

In silent room, a chair squeaks loud,
The cat's a ghost, but feels so proud.
With every creak, the shadows dance,
Old socks still dream of daring romance.

The fridge hums tunes of yesterday,
While dust bunnies join the ballet.
Footsteps echo, ghosts take a bow,
Time just laughs, like a sly old cow.

Calendar pages flip and spin,
Declaring a battle we can't win.
With wrinkles growing upon our skin,
The couch is comfy, let's dive in.

As shadows play their funny game,
I'll forget my age, but not my name.
In this quiet hall of giggling time,
Life's a rhythm, and I'm the rhyme.

Years Encapsulated in Stillness

The clock ticks loud, a battle drum,
It tells old tales of where we're from.
Up on the shelf, the dust grows proud,
Each speck a story, whispered loud.

A loaf of bread waits, moldy and gray,
Like the good old days, it's gone astray.
The old rug chuckles, does the cha-cha,
While the cat yawns, like a big ol' ma.

Time likes to hang out, sipping tea,
While I chase memories that won't flee.
Behind my back, they sneak away,
With a wink, they're off, come what may.

In rooms where silence boldly lies,
The echo of laughter never dies.
Years may pass with little thrill,
Yet here's to time, with humor still.

The Fading Whispers of Dawn

Morning creeps in, a sleepy glow,
The coffee pot gurgles, just so slow.
Sunlight stretches, yawning wide,
While dreams run off like they've just spied.

Birds chirp loudly, like they've a plan,
To set the world ablaze, oh man!
The toast pops up, wearing a grin,
As if to say, 'Let's do this again!'

Time's a prankster, what a jest!
Each dawn unravels like a jest.
With giggles hidden in the light,
We dance on shadows, what a sight!

So, let the whispers spin their tale,
Of morning mischief, strong and frail.
In laughter's arms, we claim our crown,
As day unfolds in a silly gown.

The Fabric of Forgotten Time

Threads of yesterday weave with a grin,
Stitching together where we've been.
Old photos smile, their colors fade,
Reminding us of the pranks we played.

In pockets of laughter, secrets hide,
While memories giggle, they never bide.
The old clock sighs, 'Where's the fun?'
As I trip over something I've done.

Grandpa's old chair rocks, keeping pace,
With tales of a long-lost race.
The fabric frays at every seam,
But still it tells of a wacky dream.

Old socks in a drawer, mismatched with flair,
Dance like they're free, without a care.
As time weaves on with quirky glee,
Let's laugh at the threads that set us free.

The Veil of Dust and Days

Dust bunnies dance in the light,
Whispering what's out of sight.
I trip on the tales they weave,
Childhood giggles, they deceived.

Time's calendar sways on the wall,
A crooked reminder, we're all small.
Socks that vanished in the wash,
Waving at me, an odd nosh.

Yesterday's lunch left a trace,
Looks a bit like a fuzzy face.
Memories stuck to the floor,
Who knew snacks had so much in store?

The clock giggles as minutes run,
Telling secrets of silly fun.
Under layers of calendar haze,
Time serves us laughter in waves.

Fragments in the Attic

In the attic, what treasures lie?
A hat that makes my cat sigh.
Old toys that sprout dust with flair,
Speaking stories of forgotten care.

A clown from a carnival past,
Wobbles around, laughter amassed.
With each creak of the floorboard loud,
I'm the jester, playing for a crowd.

Boxes of letters, some torn and yellow,
Love notes written by a forgotten fellow.
Each one brings a chuckle, a smile,
Reminds me to stay a while.

Fragments of time like a jigsaw fit,
A puzzle of giggles where memories sit.
In the attic's embrace so grand,
I'm the keeper of laughter's brand.

The Halos of History

History's hats hang on hooks,
Dancing around like storybooks.
Each hat a character, bizarre and bright,
Whispering tales of the silliest plight.

Ancient scrolls with doodles abound,
Codifying laughter is how we're bound.
Caesar's wig that flies with glee,
"Remember me for my spaghetti!"

The knights in armor, clinking so loud,
Chasing chickens in a knightly crowd.
Their battle cries turn into roast,
Who knew that history could boast?

Halos that twinkle with each laugh,
Reminding us to enjoy the craft.
In every era, funny tales rise,
Time's a jest, in disguise.

Memories Suspended in Air

In the living room, memories hang,
Like awkward photos of a family sang.
I'm sure that parrot could talk back,
Recalling moments we'd love to hack.

Strings of old holiday lights aglow,
Twinkling with laughter from long ago.
Each flicker a wink from the past,
How those gatherings flew by so fast.

Cookies that burned, but we still cheered,
Thanks to the dog, who was not endeared.
Under the table, he'd take a bite,
And we'd burst into giggles, what a sight!

Memories, like bubbles, float everywhere,
Each one a burst of love and care.
Suspended in air, with a wink and a sway,
Time's humor brightens up our way.

Hiding in the Corners of Time

In the corner, dust bunnies play,
Chasing shadows, hip-hop hooray!
Tick-tock tickles in the air,
While the old clock just stands there.

Socks disappear, what a joke!
Sneaky gremlins, or just smoke?
Time slips on banana peels,
As laughter up and down it squeals.

A cat naps on the calendar,
Dreaming of fish and a chandelier.
Minutes giggle, seconds tease,
As the sun takes a whimsical breeze.

With each hour, surprises sprout,
Old age laughs and then shouts out.
In the corners, mischief thrives,
In the dance of our silly lives.

Dust Motions in the Sunlight

Dancing dusty, particles prance,
In sunbeams, they twirl and chance.
Like little fairies on a spree,
Waving 'hello' to you and me.

Each motes' a story, held so tight,
Whispering secrets of day and night.
Chasing laughter, chasing dreams,
Through window panes and playful beams.

A sneeze sends them on a quest,
Making chaos at their best!
As sunlight starts to fade away,
They have a dance-off, just for play.

With the dusk, they all retreat,
Counting twinkles, it's quite the feat.
In tomorrow's glow, they will return,
To spin again in their dust-filled turn.

The Inkwell of Enchantment

Once a pen, now a magic wand,
Inkwells bubble, prompt and respond.
Words doodle doodles, giggle and slip,
As they sail on an ink-splashing trip.

A story leaks of dragons and gnomes,
With sock puppets in riveting tomes.
Plot twists woven like a sweet surprise,
Oh, how the scribbles dance and rise!

A hiccup bursts a bubble of rhyme,
Ink blots blossoming, having a good time.
Laughter echoes on every page,
These scribbled tales hold wit and sage.

The quill dips low, then takes to flight,
Spinning yarns until it's night.
Inkwells hold more than just ink,
They cradle chaos—what do you think?

Unraveling the Fabric of Our Days

Threads of color, woven tight,
Fraying slowly, it's quite a sight.
Each day's a stitch, a world so grand,
With tangled yarn in every hand.

A kitty leaps through the fabric, oh!
Chasing a tail, in time's great show.
A patch of laughter, a patch of tears,
Stitching together our hopes and fears.

Time's needle pokes, and what a spree,
We unravel chaos, like a quilted sea.
As we laugh and stitch again,
Recreating every silly den!

Through the warp and weft, we prance,
In a hodgepodge of a whimsical dance.
Finding joy in every fray,
As moments fade and fade away.

The Clock's Embrace

Tick-tock, it dances, never a break,
In a fluff of dust, a ticklish quake.
Time wears a hat, oh such a delight,
It whispers my secrets, all through the night.

Pasta on Sunday, it's always on cue,
But pizza arrives, and the clock says, "Whew!"
Baking and timing, quite the charade,
Yet here comes the cat, and plans will fade.

The hourglass winks, what a sly little fop,
Saying, "You should really hurry, don't stop!"
Could it be mocking, a tickled old chap?
Or perhaps just a friend with a drowsy nap?

With every chime, a grinning face glows,
Dance on the walls, it's a comedy show.
Time plays the jester, swirling and free,
In this clock's embrace, who'll help me pee?

Whispers of the Ancient Beams

In dusty corners where echoes reside,
The beams hold laughter, oh how they've tried!
Once they were young with stories to share,
Now they creak boldly, but don't have a care.

Whispers of legends and tales gone awry,
The chair's been known to make a man fly!
Or crack like a joke, at just the right time,
While squirrels plot mischief, a grand little crime.

Sometimes they chatter, in the dead of night,
Of a sock that vanished, oh what a fright!
Old toys come to life, under moon's funny grin,
In secrets they share, such mischief begins!

So gather 'round closely, lend me your ear,
For the laughter that's hidden, is so very near.
Amongst the ancient, the wise, the absurd,
Is joy in the whispers, oh haven't you heard?

Echoes of a Timeworn Story

Once upon a time, the tales start to trail,
With heroes who stumble and dragons that fail.
The prince lost his shoe, or so goes the tale,
Wishing on stars, as the legends unveil.

Socks made of clouds, a hat quite absurd,
The hero forgot and that's just the word.
He tripped over laughter, oh what a sound,
Where echoes of stories bounce all around.

Witches bake cookies with wands made of twigs,
While owls hoot loudly, and dance like they're pigs.
Every turn of a page, brings giggles and grins,
In echoes of stories, it's where fun begins!

So if you are willing to suspend your own doubt,
Join the echoes of laughter, there's never a drought.
These timeworn tales cheer and embrace,
With each little giggle, they lighten the space.

The Sigh of Forgotten Days

Once were the moments, now a fresh breeze,
With pillows of laughter, it's such a tease.
Forgotten days volley, each one a jest,
Like socks with no matches, a very fine quest.

Twirling round memories, they giggle with glee,
As if time were a dog, chasing its flea.
The sun wears a grin, as the moon rolls its eyes,
For what's better than sunny spots, oh my, what a rise!

Old chairs creak stories, of naps gone astray,
"Once I was snoring; now look at me play!"
Ticklish and happy, the days danced away,
In sighs of forgotten, come join the buffet!

So gather your smiles, let them flutter and glide,
In the beauty of nonsense, classically wide.
With every sigh echoing, laughter takes flight,
What's gone is now funny, let's party tonight!

Secrets Kept in the Walls

Whispers flutter like moths at night,
Secrets creep from left to right.
Old shoes hiding from the dust,
Laughing at us, they must!

Noses twitch at walls so silent,
Cracks reveal tales, quite defiant.
Forgotten socks, a cheery pair,
Making mischief with no care!

Pipes groan stories of past meals,
Telling secrets with squeaky squeals.
Even the shadows dance and play,
Debating what to steal today!

Who knew walls could chat so well?
Each crevice hides a jolly spell.
In the corners, laughter rings,
Tickling us with silly things!

The Lattice of Lost Dreams

Behind the curtains, dreams collide,
Riding on waves of rollercoaster pride.
A kite once flew, now stuck in a tree,
Grumbling softly, "Why not me?"

A pot of gold turned into clay,
Lost adventure with nothing to say.
Yet fears and giggles manage to bloom,
Bouncing around in the dusty room!

Crayons miss sketching childhood's plans,
Instead, they're playing in dustpan bands.
Yesterday's laughter hangs in the air,
As memories wiggle without a care!

A treasure map marked with no 'X',
Just doodles left, waiting for checks.
If only those dreams came out to play,
Oh, what fun they'd have today!

Hues of Yesterday's Light

Colors drip like spilled paint spills,
Creating joy amidst the ills.
A banana-yellow laugh we adore,
With shades of pink on the back door!

Laughter echoes in shades of green,
Echoing memories of all that's been.
Crisp blue skies teasing us still,
While the clock ticks, always will.

Dust bunnies dance in purple haze,
Feeling festive in their lazy ways.
Oh, to catch their frolicking flight,
Would surely turn frowns to light!

Walls flaunted splashes, bright and bold,
Telling tales of love untold.
In every corner, a memory gleams,
Living freely in all our dreams!

Chronicles of the Overhead Beams

Beams of wood with stories to share,
Wobble a bit, but they don't care.
Hanging like pals with a casual grin,
Timbers whispering, "Let's begin!"

From spider webs to squeaky floors,
Every creak's a memory that soars.
Lifetimes of laughter sealed with glue,
In every crack, a joke or two!

Old hats dangle like forgotten stars,
While the moon peeks through plain old bars.
It's a party where the planks can sway,
And hidden giggles won't fade away!

So here's to beams and tales they trod,
Reminders of mischief from the odd.
In every splinter, a giggle lies,
Wishing to soar in the midnight skies!

Echoes in the Hallway

Footsteps shuffle down the lane,
Echoes giggle, no one's sane.
A cat in a hat, prancing about,
Chasing shadows, laughing out.

Pictures trapped in frames of gold,
Whisper secrets, tales retold.
Once they danced, now they just stare,
Waving back from their comfy chair.

Chandeliers swing, a waltz of dust,
Cups on a shelf begin to rust.
A mouse in socks slides down the wall,
Join the party, let's have a ball!

A clock that ticks with attitude,
Winks at time, plays the rude.
Moments twirl in jazzy jive,
Here in the hallway, all alive!

The Lullaby of Ages

Cradles rock, and snore with cheer,
Old socks dance with wine and beer.
Toys of yonder give a sigh,
Balloons float, the goodbyes fly.

Dust bunnies boogie 'round the room,
In their disco ball of gloom.
A rocking chair breaks out in song,
While the world outside just hums along.

Time, it seems, wears silly hats,
Sipping tea with chirpy bats.
A grandfather clock, clocking in late,
Rummaging snacks from an old crate.

Chaos reigns with jellybeans,
Silly games of ghostly dreams.
A lullaby with a hiccup twist,
In the embrace of a time-warped mist.

Footprints on the Floorboards

Sneaky feet with muddy shoes,
Leave their mark in funny hues.
The floorboards creak a silly tune,
Bouncing back like a loony balloon.

A pair of slippers starts to prance,
As if they're leading a silly dance.
Each footprint tells a jolly jest,
In this place where laughter's a quest.

Cats leave pawprints, oh so bold,
Magic tales of mischief told.
And ghosts play tag in bright moonlight,
With giggles echoing through the night.

Wooden planks whisper many tales,
Of playful pies and moonlit trails.
In each creak, a chuckle breeds,
Amidst the stories and the deeds!

Threads of Yesterday

Socks in knots and ties gone wild,
Woven stories, humor styled.
A patchwork quilt shares secrets neat,
Of mishaps and moments bittersweet.

The cotton candy dreams we spun,
A tapestry, not just for fun.
Button eyes blink in goofy shock,
Fabric giggles, tick tock, tick tock.

Threads unravel, tickle the toes,
While the past prances, and time doze.
A needle laughs at all the fuss,
Stitching together a joyful bus.

Memories drawn in colors bright,
Filling the air with pure delight.
In the weave, we find our place,
Funny tales time can't erase.

Reflections in a Dusty Mirror

In the mirror, dust does dance,
A hint of laughter, a strange romance.
I see my hair, it waves goodbye,
As if it's planning to learn to fly.

An old sock lies behind the chair,
It seems to giggle without a care.
The clock's hands spin, a playful swirl,
Tick-tock giggles, in quiet whirl.

A rogue shoe hides beneath the bed,
With tales of travels, dreams it's fed.
Each tickle of dust, a joke unspooled,\nIn candid moments, sanity ruled.

Time's prankster, playing with my mind,
In a world where chaos is well-defined.
A grin pops forth, through time we race,
With memories flying, lids on their face.

The Silence of Forgotten Rooms

In rooms where whispers used to play,
Dust bunnies frolic, they've found their way.
Each shadow hides a giggling ghost,
Of laundry piles we dread the most.

A chair remembers the creak of laughter,
While the cat's plotting a sly disaster.
Old books chuckle in riddles deep,
As silence creeps, the secrets keep.

The curtains sway, a dance of glee,
They tease the chairs, 'Come join in free.'
Oh the floors, with squeaks that dare,
To share old stories, without a care.

Hidden treasures in crannies reside,
With echoes of childhood, laughter in stride.
Time winks at us, a cheeky sprite,
In forgotten rooms, we find pure delight.

Memories in the Corners

In corners where cobwebs hold their sway,
Old toys chuckle, still ready to play.
An engine's roar or a doll's sweet giggle,
In every shadow, they peek and wiggle.

Dust motes swirl like confetti bright,
A parade of moments, fluttering light.
Old photographs wink from their place,
With silly faces, they join the chase.

Boxes stacked high with mismatched dreams,
Unfurling tales, or so it seems.
A sock puppets laugh amidst the gloom,
While mismatched pairs yearn for their room.

In these corners, stories collide,
With echoes of joy, we cannot hide.
Time's silly antics bring smiles anew,
With memories tucked in, just for a view.

A Tapestry of Seasons

Winter whispers with frosty breath,
While spring chuckles, defying death.
Autumn leaves laugh as they swirl down,
Summer's sunshine wears a golden crown.

A quilt of colors sewn with care,
Time twirls in circles, a light-hearted fare.
Each patch a memory, a moment we've spun,
In this tapestry, we've all had fun.

Seasons teeter, dance, and sway,
In the warmth of laughter, they find their way.
Time takes a peek from a sunny nook,
With a grin that says, 'Come, let's play hook!'

Each shift of light and shade we see,
Is nature's joke, a cosmic spree.
In this vibrant weave, we shall delight,
A silly riddle in day and night.

The Ghosts That Live Here

They dance in the kitchen, all covered in dust,
With sandwiches flying, a ghostly crust.
They laugh over tea, it's quite the delight,
Making toast in the air, oh what a sight!

One ghost in pajamas, a sight to behold,
Whispers of secrets, oh how they've told!
They argue with shadows, it's a real showdown,
Who knew ghosts played cards, with such a frown!

And when dinner is served, they feast out of sight,
With clattering cutlery, it's a comical night.
The chandelier swings, as they chatter and scheme,
These ghosts throw a party, just like in a dream!

So if you hear giggles, don't fret nor despair,
It's just all the phantoms having fun in the air.
Banish your worries, embrace all the cheer,
For the ghosts that live here are simply sincere!

Patterns Woven by Time

In a tapestry woven of laughter and cheer,
The threads are our moments from yesteryear.
There's one with a cat that just wouldn't behave,
And another of socks that went missing, oh grave!

Time spins the fabric, oh what a design,
With clumsy old uncles and lost Valentine.
There's a pattern of mishaps, both silly and grand,
Like a clown with a pie that was perfectly planned!

From ties that were crooked to hairdos that flopped,
Each stitch tells a story, where laughter just popped.
A swirl of confusion with mischief entwined,
In patches of joy that we've all left behind.

So let's toast to the weaves of our curious fate,
For time makes us silly as we decorate.
With colors of whimsy, let us reminisce,
In this fabric of fun, don't you dare miss!

Muffled Footfalls of Yesteryears

The floor creaks with laughter, a ghostly ballet,
As echoes of footfalls lead the way to play.
Each step is a whisper, a grunt, and a jump,
As memories mingle—oh, what a thump!

In slippers of silence, they shuffle so slow,
Waltzing through hallways, as if in a show.
They stumble on cat toys, chuckling with glee,
These muffled footfalls are happy, you see!

They moonwalk on hardwood, then trip on a rug,
Creating a symphony, a soft little hug.
With giggles they frolic, misty and spry,
Leaving trails of laughter as they float by.

So if you should listen, with heart open wide,
You'll hear little footfalls that giggle and slide.
Through corridors bright, let joy be your guide,
For yesteryears whisper, with laughter beside.

Fables of the Past

Gather 'round children, for stories of old,
Of fables and legends where laughter unfolds.
There's a tale of a chicken who dreamed of a flight,
Who danced with the stars every magical night!

Then there's that old king with a crown made of cheese,
Who ruled with a hiccup and sent shivers with sneeze.
His jester, a kitten, with antics so spry,
Made all of his subjects just giggle and sigh!

With quirks of mischief, and puns that run deep,
These fables remind us to chuckle and leap.
So raise up your glasses, let tales spin around,
For laughter is timeless, in every sound!

In the realm of the past, let fun be the light,
Where stories of joy make the heart feel so bright.
So cherish these moments, the giggles and glee,
For fables of joy set our spirits all free!

The Stirrings of Forgotten Hours

Tick-tock goes the clock on the wall,
Each chime sends memories large and small.
Lost socks wander in time's great race,
Chasing their pairs at a brisk, funny pace.

Grandpa's jokes echo, but no one laughs,
They've heard them so often, like old worn-out calfs.
Yet every tick brings a grin to the face,
Of moments so silly, in this timeless space.

Doodles from yesterday float in the air,
Marking the spot of a gone-out hair.
The cat has a party with shadows and beams,
Plotting wild adventures that break at the seams.

So here we sit with time astray,
Laughing at clocks that forgot the day.
In a world that spins a bit askew,
The fun of lost hours refreshes us too.

Lullabies of Lost Seasons

Spring's petunias giggle in seasonal pranks,
While wintery snowmen rehearse funny thanks.
Summer's grilling oddities rise in the air,
As autumn's leaves dance without a care.

The melodies of sunshine in hats made of pie,
Create silly tunes that cause butterflies to fly.
In the background, frogs compete to croak right,
They harmonize loudly, as they give it a fright.

So gather round folks, for the great jamboree,
Where seasons wear costumes, so wild and free.
We'll laugh with the daisies and tiptoe through ants,
In a world where humor prances and plants.

Unruly raindrops join in for the fun,
Raining down laughter rather than done.
With memories spun from the past like a kite,
We'll dance through the seasons until the night.

When the Clock Winks

A clock on the wall gives a cheeky little wink,
As hours stumble over, not quite sure what to think.
Every tick shows off a little mishap,
Like pancakes sticking in a morning flap!

Minute hands do the cha-cha with flair,
While second hands race without a care.
Time plays peek-a-boo, silly and spry,
As we giggle at hours that flutter on by.

The sun jumps high, then plays hide-and-seek,
Casting shadows that jiggle and squeak.
Time's a prankster with tricks up its sleeve,
Pulling our legs, we hardly believe!

Tickles from laughter echo through the halls,
When the clock's jolly spirit dances and calls.
So let's toast to moments that giggle and shine,
For life's a caper where silly meets time.

The Archive of Daydreams

In a cupboard of dreams, where the silly reside,
Witty thoughts bubble and never hide.
A puppy in pajamas snores loud as a train,
While secrets of laughter giggle like rain.

Hats of imagination float up on the shelf,
Filled with the hopes of a whimsical elf.
Clouds made of marshmallows drift in and out,
With whispers of joy, that leave us in doubt.

Monkeys in bowties recite silly prose,
Sprinkling fairy dust where the laughter flows.
Through the archive we traverse, what joy, what cheer,
In the land of the dreams, we chase without fear.

So here's to the tales where nonsense is art,
An archive of daydreams that tickles the heart.
Let's open the doors to forever play,
And fondly remember the fun of today!

Faint Traces of Laughter

In the attic, dust bunnies play,
Old socks tell tales of yesterday.
A cat on a shelf, so full of sass,
Chasing shadows and moments past.

Grandpa's chair starts to creak and groan,
Whispers of chuckles fill the zone.
A rubber chicken hides in the night,
Wondering when it'll take flight.

The clock on the wall seems to grin,
Counting the giggles from way back when.
Tick-tock goes the hand, so sly,
Bringing forth laughter, oh my, oh my!

So here we sit with a grin so wide,
As echoes of humor we cannot hide.
For within these walls, joy leaves its mark,
Like glow-in-the-dark stickers after dark.

Between the Cracks of Daylight

A misfit sandwich lost in a drawer,
Plans for a feast turned into folklore.
Socks in a battle for matching fate,
Yearn for the moment to celebrate.

Sunlight dances as it sneaks through,
Chasing the dust with a playful view.
Behind the curtains, a shadow slips,
Trying to pirouette, doing flips.

The broom stands still, a knight in repose,
Guarding the laughter that no one knows.
A comedy play from last week's attempt,
Fell flat on the floor with a loud preempt.

Yet in the cracks of each shining day,
Jokes linger softly, never to stray.
As we chuckle, inside we know,
The funny side is where memories grow.

Subtle Murmurs of History

The old photo album grins with delight,
Tangled hair days caught in the light.
Uncle Bob's dance, a sight to behold,
In the family feast, he stole the gold.

Whispers of times that seemed to flake,
Remind us of pies that we dared not bake.
A dog in a bonnet, what a fine trend,
Each snapshot an uproar, a laugh to lend.

Grandma's old recipes, blurry and worn,
Attempted disasters, singing and scorned.
Yet each plop and clatter brings forth a grin,
Who knew that burnt toast could echo within?

So we gather these stories, silly and sweet,
In the murmur of history, laughter takes seat.
A tribute to chaos mixed with a twist,
As time stands still, we add to the list.

The Undercurrent of Time

Tick-tock, tick-tock, the clock's lumbering gait,
Holds secrets of jokes that accumulate weight.
With each passing hour, a memory's tease,
As the cat plots revenge on the dog with ease.

Jars of old candy, appears intact,
But the licorice stares back with a history, I'm cracked!
A spoonful of sugar makes it seem fine,
While laughter bubbles invisible wine.

The carpet is sprawled with mismatched socks,
Pretending they're penguins, forming a flock.
As the furniture chuckles and shifts with glee,
We dance like no one's watching, carefree as can be.

In this realm of whimsy, the moments entwine,
Echoes of laughter are always divine.
So let's toast to the shenanigans yet to unfold,
In the undercurrent of time, life stories are told.

Tides of Memory

In a suitcase old, I found a sock,
A relic from days when I was a jock.
It smelled like dreams and forgotten laughter,
But now it's a tale, and I'm the master.

A sandwich from lunch, a crusty old bite,
In a time capsule, it gave me a fright.
It whispered of picnics, of ketchup and fun,
Now it's a moldy, mysterious bun!

My diary spills secrets of crushes and schemes,
Of doodles and doodads, of popcorn dreams.
But every page turned feels like a riddle,
As my handwriting? Oh dear! It's a fiddle!

Yet laughter drifts in, like a breeze full of cheer,
As I dive into memory, year after year.
With each silly mishap, oh what a delight,
Time's a comedian, keeping us bright!

Gazing Through Yesterday's Windows

Peering through glasses, two lenses so thick,
I see silly moments that make my heart tick.
A cat in a hat, singing in tune,
Oh, how bizarre—was that last June?

Frames full of snapshots, mischief's delight,
Blurry faces laughing, oh what a sight!
An umbrella that flipped in a sudden wind gust,
Now, it's a tale filled with solo trust.

The clock on the wall stops when time's feeling fun,
Tick-tock transforms into a race just begun.
Chasing my memories, I laugh and I soar,
In the gallery of time, who could ask for more?

So raise your glass high to the moments we chase,
With a wink from the past, let's enjoy this space.
We're all just reflections in a puddle of glee,
Dancing through time, just being silly me!

A Gathering of Echoes

Echoes of laughter dance in the hall,
Where socks go missing, oh that's the ball!
A cacophony of giggles, a raucous delight,
As shadows do shuffle, then vanish from sight.

Whispers of blunders hang in the air,
As toast once adored, became quite the affair.
Burnt edges and crumbs, we all had a share,
Now it's legend—my friends, do beware!

The walls hold our stories, the ups and the downs,
Of silly mishaps, and runaway clowns.
A parade of antics through each creaky seam,
Life's just a circus, with laughable themes!

So gather your echoes, let's cherish the noise,
Fill the air with laughter, glimmering joys.
For time may keep moving, yet here's the key,
In the grand show of life, we're wild and carefree!

The Chronicles of Ordinary Shadows

Once upon a time, in a land full of dust,
Lived shadows that giggled, oh what a must!
Tripping on moonbeams with tap-dancing feet,
In a quirky ballet, they couldn't be beat.

The toaster once told tales of overcooked bread,
Of mornings and jam that danced in your head.
And the fridge sang softly of ice cream's great fate,
As shadows debated the hour to sate.

With a breeze through the curtains, they spun with delight

Drawing cartoons in the soft, morning light.
Every mishap echoed like a sweet symphony,
As ordinary shadows danced so whimsically.

So let's celebrate moments that flicker and sway,
And cherish these stories that brighten our day.
For in the mundane, there's magic we find,
As shadows weave tales, causing giggles unconfined!

www.ingramcontent.com/pod-product-compliance
Lightning Source LLC
Chambersburg PA
CBHW060145230426
43661CB00003B/579